THE ALL + FLESH

THE ALL + FLESH

BRANDI BIRD

POEMS

ANANSI

Published in Canada in 2023 and the USA in 2023 by House of Anansi Press Inc.
houseofanansi.com

House of Anansi Press is committed to protecting our natural environment. This book is made of material from well-managed FSC®-certified forests, recycled materials, and other controlled sources.

House of Anansi Press is a Global Certified Accessible™ (GCA by Benetech) publisher. The ebook version of this book meets stringent accessibility standards and is available to readers with print disabilities.

27 26 25 24 23   1 2 3 4 5

Library and Archives Canada Cataloguing in Publication

Title: The all + flesh / Brandi Bird.
Other titles: all plus flesh | all and flesh
Names: Bird, Brandi, author.
Description: Poems.
Identifiers: Canadiana (print) 2023019768X | Canadiana (ebook) 20230197698
ISBN 9781487011826 (softcover) | ISBN 9781487011833 (EPUB)
Classification: LCC PS8603.I7265 A75 2023 | DDC C811/.6—dc23

Book design: Greg Tabor
Cover image/artwork: Kris Leov

House of Anansi Press is grateful for the privilege to work on and create from the Traditional Territory of many Nations, including the Anishinabeg, the Wendat, and the Haudenosaunee, as well as the Treaty Lands of the Mississaugas of the Credit.

 Canada Council   Conseil des Arts
for the Arts   du Canada

ONTARIO ARTS COUNCIL
CONSEIL DES ARTS DE L'ONTARIO
an Ontario government agency
un organisme du gouvernement de l'Ontario

With the participation of the Government of Canada
Avec la participation du gouvernement du Canada | Canadä

We acknowledge for their financial support of our publishing program the Canada Council for the Arts, the Ontario Arts Council, and the Government of Canada.

Printed and bound in Canada

Dedicated to my dad, my first storyteller.

TABLE OF CONTENTS

THE ALL + FLESH

POEM FOR WHITE PEOPLE

Circle, spiral, circle, spiral.

NDN compartmentalization.

I live in the shack my grandpa built after WWII.

Drive to Selkirk in the middle of the night.

I hold a black-and-white photo from the 30s of my grandma on Brokenhead First Nation.

Say *holay*.

Flick a camo-print lighter.

I put bars on the windows.

Study this low-income housing complex & the bread truck that visits on Sundays.

KFC for my eighth birthday in Kildonan Park.

Merle Haggard's "Branded Man."

My mom's perfume called *Opium*.

Restraining order after restraining order after restraining order, my mom stalking my dad in 1995.

I look for an enfranchised great uncle dead on the Métis Veterans' Memorial Monument.

Go to Child & Family Services
sessions in court, be Permanent Ward.

I kiss a girl at 15.

Sleep in the back seat while my
mom's boyfriend runs cocaine.

I don't live on my territory.

Imitate my dad's accent.

Write about my territory even
though I can't afford to go home.

This I'm not going to say.

Be density.

I smoke with pneumonia.

Air.

Use the cognitive science degree I
never got.

Water.

Skip my great-grandma's funeral on
Pine Creek First Nation.

The first language I ever learned.

I walk by the Adam Beach mural in
downtown Winnipeg.

My kokum calls Stephen Harper
a snake.

The muddy banks of the Red
River.

Hold a residential school
settlement for fourteen
thousand dollars.

I fall asleep while my dad sings
Johnny Cash.

Ignore my auntie yelling out the
window of her old Chevy.

Imagine my grandpa's shotgun
pointed at my dad in 1993.

Imagine my grandma singing with
Hank Williams in the '40s.

Shoot a water pistol full of vodka
into my mouth.

I get a one-year membership to
Ancestry.com.

I tattoo syllabics on my wrist
for one hundred dollars.

Read about my brother's dad going
to jail for 20 years for smuggling
weapons over the border.

Plant the flag, grow it out of
my back.

I was born with dark hair &
darker eyes.

Be NDN time.

I get free admission to the MOA.

Think [Name Redacted], [Name
Redacted], [Name Redacted],
[Name Redacted].

Circle, spiral, circle, spiral.

COUNTDOWN AS DRUNK MOTHERS

After Michael Wasson & Danez Smith

10. Somewhere, winter:
      A girl's tableau of snow angels
            halos added later
                       made of sticks & tinsel from the dumpster

9. January blue. Girls play for twelve hours
      because they can't go home

8. The snow piles where the plows push it
      & girls slide down hills into the sleeping street

7. Girls' mothers drunk at nine a.m.

6. Cheque day
      nicotine yellow
           lasting until the sun sets

5. Over the horizon
      Grab my hand

4. Cold fingers in the dark
      a bottle of Budweiser
          & a snowball

3. Drunk mother or child
      wanting to go home

2. Low-income townhouses.
      Girls' braids like barbed wire

1. Girls spitting out baby teeth
      alone in the snow

0. A history
      of beer vendors
           a collapse

BURNT

For Tanner

My brother twists the grinder, a joint
    lit in his childhood bedroom (painted blue). His bottle-
        green eyes track the way history has moved through holes
in the walls. The holes lead nowhere. They lead down, sharp
& shy with knowledge like the ruddy skin of a slap
    fading fast. I want him to know the difference between obligation
        & willingness. One tastes burnt. One tastes like burning. Learn
the difference between charcoal & the wood when it hits
the fire. My brother doesn't know he is a story without
    an end. The spirit of an ending in the way smoke drifts from his
    mouth as he laughs, a tilt in the world, twin-curved glass.
        The futures that happen in all worlds & none of them.
    My brother, a man but younger than me. So new.
        His lips burn on weed ash & the words he doesn't speak
to me or anyone. He swallows them like Prozac
    on the days he remembers to take it. I wonder what he thinks about
    this poem. If he dreams about windows & sees holes
in the sky, a way out or maybe a way through time. A place I couldn't write
    even if I lived there. The way I can't comprehend even my own death
    or the possibility that I will die like the feeling of my
grandmother's hands on mine. The feeling of my hands on my brother's.
    I ghost through life & he phantoms.
    He sinks into smoke.
    He disappears.

VOMIT MANIFESTO

Memorize Rilke, translation: *Every angel is terrifying*.

I open my mouth & can't control what comes out.

Fold my arm into Ezekiel's wheels, rip them apart, levitate.

Collect pelts from roadkill & turn them into sculptures in my own image.

The pelts rot & a map of my body erases itself from this page.

A flood, a riptide, a nausea.

My arms & legs circle in water.

God is there & He vomits bile into the ocean.

I feel His pain in my throat & I'm taken by it.

What tradition do I replicate, do I reject?

I am as confused as you are.

God floats with me.

Why not grab His hand?

I swallow salt water, get sick, vomit.

In His image, I degrade myself.

Make my body unlivable so God disappears too.

I'm alone & grow itchy wings, tear them out at the root.

I stay terrestrial, accelerated by the earth.

Grief, a synonym for pain. *Every angel is terrifying*.

Grief turns over in bed & wants me to visit in its dreams.

Is a halo over every word I write.

Grief says: *Be not afraid* & I still am.

There is power in fear too.

It's how I survive.

THE ALL + FLESH

thirst / sweet morning breath / I
swallow jardiance / metformin /
glyburide /a needle's hand / slow
/ spills wellness in reach / this die-
off-of cells /a cull of insulin / is
an argument too / watch me argue
with the past / the room in which
I burn sage / & think good thoughts /
has a hole in the roof & I keep chasing
birds / out of their nests / I find chicks
on the floorboards / abandoned / by
their mothers / no longer alive / my
mother doesn't know / I'm sick /
she will now / picture the pump
/ the soak through the room /
where I come to be alone / thirst
in abundance / starvation / abundance
/ rebellion against witness / doctor /
mother / my stomach asks for clarity
/ a diagnosis of yes or no / good or bad
/ the all + flesh / I am made of centuries
& carbohydrates / molars cut/ hunger
grew / with me since childhood / I can't
escape the mouths of others / the hands of
others / so I give up trying / I eat a hole in the
roof / of this house & in all my good dresses / I
am not frugal or pious or godly / I eat / I eat /
until my mouth needles / the dark

A GLOSSARY OF ILLNESS

After Eve Tuck & C. Ree

What if all possible
pain was only the grief of truth?
—Brenda Shaughnessy

ABSOLUTE

That which is total. A whole. Incomparable. No metaphor can touch me.

APPETITE

To crave is a verb & it beats arrhythmically. Does your chest hurt? Tell me where it hurts.

COMPLAINT

I wake up one morning & I can feel my body for the first time. I'm nauseous & it overtakes me. My shadow flickers on the wall, the arc of the ceiling bending me into unnatural shapes. I want to write about this but I have no words through the feeling. How do you write without thought? On instinct alone, propelled by physical sensation? I want to write about my pain but it's been made real enough already, a clay sculpture fired & broken.

DEGRADATION

A year and a half of illness & no answers. No one takes me seriously until I lose *x* pounds in a month. Degradation is the decline of empires or just one body. My body is not an empire but first contact happened at birth. The doctor pulled me out of my Native mother's womb & noticed I was jaundiced. I slept under blue lights that looked like flying saucers for days. They took me away from my mother & now I try to write about how I came to be—*My parents met at a bar like Indians do, drunk on cheap beer & cheaper talk, never understanding how remarkable it was they had survived to that moment.* I have survived twenty-eight years but I know that *love is like a hand gripping a cold beer. Love holds the bottle lightly until someone tries to take it.*

FAILURE

I am expelled from university before I know I'm a writer. Bulimic & sad, I lie in bed instead of going to class & I flunk out of every class. I am so afraid of failure that I haven't written since I was fourteen. I choose to throw up everything I eat, an irony now. I remain afraid of failure but I'm more afraid of nausea, unaware that this is a type of pain until a doctor tells me to rate it from one to ten. I don't know why I never considered that it hurt in a traditional sense. I was so detached from my body that when I said *My stomach hurts* I meant my heart. I write this glossary, wrapped up in my own pain, & it's all I can think about. I fail to eat. I fail to escape the sensation. I fail to explain those feelings adequately.

HEALTHY

I am not & I have never been healthy but I've pretended. You've pretended too.

NAUSEA

I read Sartre when I was fifteen & I didn't understand any of it.
I haven't tried again. What I feel when I'm sick isn't the pain of the
amorphous. But it is truthful, which is abstract, which is different from fact,
which isn't anything I can hold on to. There is no reason, not yet. Perhaps it
is amorphous & I don't understand nausea well enough beyond the simple
experience of it. I can't write & yet I am writing. I can't & I do.

SENSATION

I have written about sensation. Pain is the sensation of touch internally.
Referred pain is the process of our internal organs throwing signals to
other parts of the body telling us something is wrong inside. When I
was fourteen, I wrote poems about suicide but never showed them to
anyone. I wrote about slaughterhouses—*the great god eye / of each dead pig
/ parallel / on every carcass*—& last year I found these poems on a long-
forgotten website. I wonder where I would be if I had kept writing &
hadn't stopped so abruptly, hadn't gotten so sick. I'm still sick & I delete
the poems from the internet, read them one last time—*at school / the
farmer's daughter / always said / that a pig's lung / could be her lung too*. I knew
even then that we breathe the same way, can transplant our organs to
each other & become new animals.

STARVATION

There is order in starvation but it is a false order. When I did it
purposely, it felt controlled, a descent on my terms. Now I drink high-
calorie protein shakes to make sure I don't pass out on campus.
I take medication that gives me headaches so I can eat three small meals

a day & I feel sorry for myself. I feel sorry. I am fat & I'm trying not to starve & other people's desire tells me that's impossible. My pharmacist tells me I look great & I have no words to explain what has happened to make me look this way. Starvation robbed me of words for twelve years. I'm afraid that will happen again. I write to you, hungry & sick at the same time. I write without process, only desperation.

ZOFRAN

As Angie Sijun Lou writes: *Not everything feels like something else.* Two hundred dollars a month for small yellow pills I cut in half so I can make them last longer. They are seed like, grow like wildflowers in my belly. They keep me from vomiting every day, keep me the same weight, or at least mostly the same weight. No more free fall. I can grasp at the walls of my brain when they work, have a coherent thought though they give me pounding headaches. I can see the shadows of my body when the sun sets but without recognition. There is only a mystery & the hours when I'm not in pain. How do you measure pain, how am I to be beautiful in my suffering? I wash the bile out of my mouth & speak plainly to you. I hurt.

BE CAREFUL WHO YOU SPEAK FOR.
IT'S ALWAYS JUST YOURSELF.

For the Health Sciences Centre's Adolescent Eating Disorder Program

When I am sixteen
                    a psychiatrist
                                   will ask
                                            Is it sexual?

Is what sexual? Me? Am I sexual? Is my mouth sexual? My teeth?

& then he places words on my tongue, and they're cacophonous in his hands.
                    He apologizes.
He chews up words at my appointments. I talk
about my mother who is dead
                    who I have killed,
                                   who is a verb
                                                that erases
                                                            herself everyday.
There is no emptiness I can't fill.

            Is it sexual?

Leave me alone.

                    I wish I had said *fuck off.*

But instead I vomit in the psychiatrist's office, words & more
            words, some that aren't even mine. He collects them

in his psychiatric notes & I get an appointment for next week.
I will never be satisfied
until I swallow
all tongues, all language,
until I suffer, start
the cycle over. I look just like my mother.
Black eyes, tan skin, moon face, spitting teeth
on the side of the highway.

EVERY DAY AFTER

Dawn of Mother nodding.

Dawn of event horizon.

Dawn of dirty child & her face turned toward the sun.

Dawn of rug burn on knees.

      A margin of error in memory.

Dawn of calico cat–fur float.

Dawn of *beautiful girl, just beautiful.*

Dawn of pullout couch on pilled carpet.

Dawn of preoccupation.

Dawn of broken tile on windowsill.

Dawn of musky smell of wood rot & soil.

      Dawn of fingers on small hips.

          Dawn of VHS in the background, *Fievel Goes West.*

            Dawn of absent fathers, hands shook.

          Dawn of invitations.

      Dawn of *body, body, body.*

Dawn of dream catchers.

      Of fitted sheet.

      Of glitter lip gloss.

      Of red.

Dawn of breath so thick she can taste it.

Dawn of silence.

Dawn of every day.

      Dawn of every day after.

          Dawn of.

MY BROTHER, AGING IN REVERSE

For Tanner

if prison is a country, let it break
        open like a clock on the hour. an escape
    of green eyes taken like child support, a boy, german-headed &
arguing with the past. innocence
     has nothing to do with it. my brother, born
        at the edge of summer, totters & falls. our mother screams
    about paternity
from the back of a pickup truck. i am not there. my brother's face
        is handsome & young & he turns eighteen & i am not
     there. the borders of his story are embellished by my voice. i am
       not invited. terra nullius in this poem, a prison is a border
of barbed wire & braided hair. our sister drives him there.
        the prairie splits like a rubber tire, burns in front
of our low-income townhouse. the car windows crack
     in the cold. a wooden bat
misses my brother's brother's
        head. those people, they just wanted to protect us
           but we hurt
    instead. we hurt & try on different clothes, new cities. my brother
on his way to visit his father in prison. we don't talk about it. i don't know
        if he will go. i just know the sweetgrass i gave my sister, tied
    with orange yarn, resting on her dash for good luck. what happens
when you are given what you never had? a gun in the back seat, no
     seatbelts, two a.m. drug run
        from kenora. this is a story i don't remember.

this is the story
i'm told. my brother in the background, a baby. he ages
in reverse. his lips split
open on new teeth & he looks
so old. if his story
is a country, i settled there.
i conquered
& brought back this poem.

STAR WITH BLASPHEMY

God was God & then He
        wasn't. I'm nine years old,
               & listening to God
tell me a story
        about the future. The future
               is a prism I hold
in my hands. A light
        shines from my chest
               & my mother's silhouette
shadows me. I'm
        trying to hide.
               from her. My palms are warm
with short lifelines, my small
        hands cracked in winter,
               reflected in God's
eyes, busy as in prayer,
        as in asking for forgiveness
               for sins I have
or have not yet committed. I come home
        from school at lunch
               to make sure my mother
isn't mad. She isn't. The sun shrinks
        around my body
               as I close the door. I cast a shadow
        in the living room & I'm saved
again & again when Jack Van Impe
        asks who will be saved at the end
               of his sermon on TV. My mother

doesn't go to church, asleep
　　　on Sundays, pills like seeds
　　　　　sprouting on the
bedroom floor. I took one once
　　　& fell asleep for a whole day
　　　　　& night,
my eyes shut, twins. I grew
　　　sunflowers
　　　　　in my sleep, flowers
with heavy heads like God
　　　looking down. He
was faceless. I couldn't tell time by Him.
　　　I just know I grew
　　　　　& grew & that night
my mother opened
　　　my bedroom door
　　　　　quiet
　　　like a star,
　　　　　closed it
　　　　　　　when I turned
　　　　　　　　　to look at her.

SYLVIA PLATH'S PILLS

Selkirk, Manitoba is the fist
   of a Native woman attached to a clock
      that counts down the days
         'til I turn sixteen. To say I left
            is a lie. My mother with bronchitis,
               her face sallow, pulls
                  a doll's string
                     down the stairs. She tossed
                     me outside
                  but the cops say I exaggerate. My police
             report is a piece of glass I find outside the bus
        depot, cloudy from shatter but the sun shines
      through. It goes in the trash
                 & I find a half-smoked cigarette
                 but I don't know how to inhale
                     yet. I hold it in my mouth & try not
                       to cough. I think I look real
                    cool in my sadness. I call my dad on a pay
                phone but he doesn't pick up.
             I steal *The Bell Jar* from the library
               & read Sylvia Plath at a Salisbury House, my mouth
   open. The red light
from the neon sign glows like diner ketchup
      & I imagine *I was, I was,*
         I was. I imagine myself as a white girl
            with a burgundy cardigan
               over my shoulders. The pills Sylvia

throws up are like stars at night,
white, disengaged from the universe.
They're useless now, wet
& disintegrating
into the dirt. I throw up every day
& imagine myself inside Sylvia's blue eyes.
I find out later
they were actually brown.

FIRES IN OCTOBER

The heat disorients me. Drought
   overflows around my body. The world will burn
      & flood & burn & flood. People
         will call the weather beautiful
            in between the rains. An Indian
               summer & the blurry sunset
                  & my father yelling at my mother
                     before he disappears. My first memory.
              He comes back again but different. He hunts
           duck & deer & moose now. He doesn't teach me
        how. The world has changed so many times
     & for the worse, for the worse. I can't imagine
   the heat getting any more bearable. I can't imagine
my voice cutting through the smoke. A season
of pilgrimage to the places that burn. Everywhere
  burns. I pray for rain & rain comes
      but it's malformed, drops explosive as a gunshot. Rain tears
         through dirt & the earth is too desperate for the sky. I am too
           desperate for the sky. To want is to leave myself open
         to anything that seems alive but isn't: flames, the ghost
      of memory, the swoon, the flood. The movement as I ignore
   the past & the future. I can't speak the present
out loud or it will transform
  into a duck flying, always flying. To live outside
    time is a gift I want to give back & the seasons
      suddenly shift. My father burns
        pinfeathers in a fire pit. I will have something
         to eat tomorrow. That should be enough.

LOVE IS DIFFERENT FROM ENDURANCE

Seizure

        of land. This settlement & abstraction. This river

& I

        are both exhausted. This *flood*

                 of the century. This *flood*

      of today.

I know

            the prairie floods

               if only

                 to hold me.

RELOCATION

ended
is a name
I've given
my body.
myself,
a church
I built
with blueprints
stolen
from
lower fort
garry.
1907,
the concept,
a calendar,
dredged
up from
a well
in the flood
of the century. north
is displacement,
the forced
removal, one
hundred
& sixty-nine
kilometres
up the prairie.

an organized
body. a body
on asphalt,
asphalt
& gravel
roads. here
there is
only
the sound
of footsteps
in rain. all ndns
are rivers, live
in the river, die
there. their bodies
float to hudson's
bay, get caught
as the river freezes,
reanimate, talk
dirty to each
other. peguis
first nation, illegal
land transfer,
moulted air
from the chimney
stack that grows
out of selkirk,
manitoba. anxiety
is summer.
is a natural

gas thermal
pump & a little
girl beside
it in 2002.
she sleeps
with a knife
under
her pillow,
a screwdriver
once
her mother
hides
the knives.
gets her hair
cut for five
dollars
at the local
barbershop
when she
gets lice.

relocated.

in wagons,
in cars,
by foot,
ticks
in armpits
& pubic

hair, tall
grasses,
tall grasses.
there are
telephone
poles that link
the whole
town to city.
to the country.
a country grows
out of
a girl's back
& she has never
known
the reserve.
permits
to leave, her
grandmother
married
on brokenhead
ojibway nation
at thirteen, children
after child
after children, herself
like fresh flint,
never struck. great-
great-grandma
tilled fields,
grew carrots,

dreamed
of owning
property,
ownership,
owning. her
sons
went to war
& one
came back
blind. he dug
his hands
into the earth.
he dug
his hands
into
the
earth.

EVERYTHING FLESH

I eat every part of you & then I settle
in the skyline. It curves

on the horizon with a tremor. Your hand on my shoulder
at a bar downtown, a direction, a verb. I want to take

liberties, make something new. Your body is a discovery, disappointing,
& I'm dizzy with the pull of a wasp's sting, again

& again, frenzied, folded in the kitchen where Pyrex flowers shake their
heads & watch. They see me see you kiss my mouth. I don't love

you. I don't close my eyes. I love myself & perhaps that is enough
of a lie to sustain me, walking shoulder to shoulder

with the sun & then the moon & your fucking hand,
always in mine. Each finger is a morsel, a thing I can suck

& I do, oh, I do. Later you cum & we eat
deer meat I bought from the market because you can't hunt.

Could you cleave me in half if you needed to?
Butcher me like I do, flesh everything, bigger than you

or me, everything, everything flesh.

BRANDI IS ALSO ALESSIO

i change my user icon on livejournal
        & girls lose track of my digital face.
                i am nowhere. know everything
        & nothing like the bald face of the moon. i invoke
moon because i'm lazy & always have been. it's easy
        to want to feel celestial when you're looking up at the sky.
                if only pixelated girls could touch
        me, feel the curve of my lips (they are winona
ryder's & i am nowhere). i invoke *nowhere*
        because girls live there.
                they don't exist in time or space, just float
        in light & change their faces, a swoon
on the internet. a girl
        anonymously accuses me of posting
                from two accounts. *brandi is also*
        alessio she writes & i feel honoured
to be mentioned at all. the internet
        makes me real & unreal. i invoke *reality*
                because shouldn't i have something to say about it?
        i have more to say about avoidance, the pith
of experience in the real world. i peel the skin
        off around my nails & my apartment stinks of cat piss.
                i am seventeen & twenty-two & thirty. i am blue
        & bleached. i am light or at least the absence
of shadow in my bedroom. i am nowhere.
        girls post about their mothers & fathers,
                post their bruised calves, post indie.
        they are post-human & so am i. profound

in our collective, a hive of girls rub themselves
      raw in real life. rug burn & then pictures of rug burn.
         i post a picture of myself crying & everything
           changes. i grow up. where am i?

RAPID TIME

Momentum into rapid
time: my body grows

from ashes of the first woman
who told me *no*. Soil

from her birthplace, her hair
falls slowly to Earth, a rope

hung from the tire swing
by the lilacs. She lived

in a shack of intimacy, children's
bodies on top

of each other at night. The forks
in the ceiling hung

buckets to catch rain & adults
slept in their own memories. Time

moves across my teeth. Time
is jagged & fast. It lodges

itself in my belly & I'm reminded
of her when I run away.

When she says I ran away.

SWELL

> From the beginning
> you should know I'm embellishing
> but was I ever twelve?
> —Sara Peters

i mythology / bite / my own arm & look / at the divots my incisors
make / rub oranges & pennies / on my best friend's face / i tell her /
it's wicca / but i just made it up / & it's astringent like the smell of her
plastic / tent in the evening before bed /

there is a pond outside / man-made / a hole / in the ground / with koi
& insects / & my friend / & I / throw tampons inside it / watch the
tampons swell & burst / into white / cotton flowers / & my friend's blue
eyes / get wide when i tell / her i've used them inside / me & i imagine /
my fingers inside / her & we fall asleep / but i am / wet / & alone / even
though she's still / right beside me /

in the morning / she tells me some girl / at school can cum / without
touch & *wow / isn't she a slut* & / the next night / i wake up / in my twin
bed / breathing heavy / from a dream / where i came / to the conclusion
that / god / isn't real but hell / still / is & i'm going there /

to die is so romantic / but to live / after death / is so dull

YOU HAVE TO GIVE UP HOPE

st jude burns beside himself
& i am going to choke
on my tongue from the force
of his club on my head

i split my body in half
& water falls to the floor
rivers in rivers
but i am lonely
although i have two parts
of myself to sew together now

the honest
work of comparing the right
& left sides of my face
one is a liar the other is a liar
too we lie to each other

& together we are aware
of our creation
we work hard
to thread the needle that will bring us
back again one as one
i am afraid to be alone
a fire above the pieces
of my skull i can't ever reach
with my hands

can pray for the dark
can close my eyes
& answer the prayers
myself

st jude forgive me
but i am not lost
i put myself here
that's my answer
to the silence that rests
in the spaces
between my body
that's my weapon
let's compare it
to yours

ARS POETICA, OR OCEAN VUONG WROTE LONELINESS IS STILL TIME SPENT WITH THE WORLD

For Zahrah

My neighbour quotes Vuong
& we both smoke
on the deck of our social
housing complex & I know
then that there is hope
until I die & then
there is other
people's
hope.

I AM TIRED OF MY MEMORY

I

Please Lord God, I
have an unpredictable
mother. The prairie
clouds over on summer days after
Sunday school & my
mother has been made
this way by the Eucharist
at Evangelical
church. A contradiction
of flesh & blood in grape juice
& rice crackers. We are not
supposed to engage
in transubstantiation
but we do it anyways. Please
forgive us.

II

Please Lord God, we
are dedicated to bad medicine. A penny
to the church, a penny
in my pocket. I want to be rich
one day but I am poor
& lying in a field by the dumpster
& the train tracks
near my house. Our pastor
talks about prosperity
like it's a transaction
& I think of Job & how his name
looks like job. I fall asleep & dream
of sunflowers
in the sky.
A train's whistle
wakes me up & for a moment
I am not myself at all.

III

Please Lord God, a neighbour
snitches when I'm too afraid
to throw out the trash one dark night. I leave
the bags in the parking lot & someone tells
the landlord. Landlords are kind of like You
but that is blasphemous & I regret
the comparison immediately. We get a warning letter
& my mother grounds me for a week. I don't see
a televangelist for seven days, the time it took
for You to create the world & even rest.

IV

Please Lord God, I dig
up mud in puddles after a storm,
creating my own world
like You. I am three years old
this time, then six, then nine.
Made out of bones, made out of the red
light I see when I look at the sun
with closed eyes. My mother yells
at me to stop. I'm getting my coat dirty
& my father is nowhere
to be found. I'll pray compulsively
to not be sent to hell.

v

Please Lord God.
This is the Gospel.
This is the Gospel.
This is the Gospel.
This is the Gospel.
This is the Gospel.
This is the Gospel.
This is the Gospel.
This is the Gospel.
This is the Gospel.
This is the Gospel.
This is the Gospel.
This is the Gospel.
This is the Gospel.
This is the Gospel.
This is the Gospel.
This is the Gospel.
This is the Gospel.
This is the Gospel.
This is the Gospel.
This is the Gospel.
This is the Gospel.
This is the Gospel.
This is the Gospel.
This is the Gospel.
This is the Gospel.
This is the Gospel.
This is the Gospel.
This is the Gospel.
This is the Gospel.

This is the narrative. This is the trajectory
toward death.

VI

Please Lord God, is hell real?
I eat my own sadness
& my mother sleeps
in the next room. My parents
created me from beer breath
& free will & I trace
my hands with chalk
on the sidewalk
outside our
townhouse. I squish
ants with my fingers
& other ants collect
their dead.

VII

Please Lord God, I am
ten years old
& praying
my soul is clean
of the Devil. I am controlled
by him & he is a man much older
than me or my father. He makes me
wake up & swear at my mother
in my head. I repent &
do it again. *Fuck you, Mom,* I think
when she falls asleep during
Jack Van Impe. She misses the chance
to save her immortal soul. There are commercials
for Folgers Coffee & Cymbalta. *Fuck you,*
Mom. We're going to hell.

VIII

Please Lord God, I pray
not to be the last
one awake. I pray
for the not. The absence
& not the bounty. I pray
for the dark room. I am afraid
to be alone.

O Lord God, how many shadows
can I name in a dark room? The many-eyed
demons, the black cats, the rabies-infected
bats? Can I rename myself
a shadow? Light arrives
slowly, morning breathing deep,
but the shadows remain.

x

Please Lord God, listen because You blessed me.
Listen because I love You.

DECLARATION

This is a statement: I was in pain

&

now I'm not. I forget pain

&

the river

forgets my hands

while I'm inside

it. How miraculous

to be ever changing

in time. A rush

into absence,

this river

flows

through a floodplain

of memory, glacial

&

otherwise. I forget

the brine

of hurt. How miraculous

to be water everywhere. Vapour

escapes

my mouth & I have lost

some dimension. I've stopped

losing

quietly. I tongue

into

the river.

I drink.

ODE TO DIABETES

God answered my prayers. Pray for sickness,
not illness. Pray to be rouge-cheeked, prayer for sweat.

Let my pancreas die. The all + flesh, pinprick of a glucometer
on my finger, trigger rosary bead, smudged insulin in my stomach fat,

medicinal clouds. A sky darkened by endocrine storms, metabolic
shock, the awe of sweat & rain. Sweet smell of piss, a perfume

called abundance worn in church when I was eleven years old in a white
dress. Pneumonia when I was twelve, my father in the oxygen

tank, breathing him, incense & rawhide. When I got better I ate
attention, praise for being alive. There is no praise now. A needle,

a sharps box, yellow asking me to slow down. I eat an apple & it spikes
my glucose. Dawn phenomena, the sun phenomena, a phenomenon

of language & its failures in the light of day. gibiskwad,
mixed gland in the anishinaabemowin medical dictionary. There is an error

in the way I speak, the way I eat. My mouth is inhuman. It curls
when I'm punished. Prayer for when I'm better, when I better

take care of myself. Prayer for hiding insulin from my father. Prayer
for the ritual at bedtime, the grip on the needle, the punc-

ture, the pump. There is no pill to dry-swallow now.
Medicine is subcutaneous. It's molten & changes form.

Insulin collects in pools like holy water I'd sneak sips of in church.
All those babies baptized in basins I put my lips on. Let God

run through me like sugar. Like He's so sweet, I'll gag.

19

I triage:
    the landscape,
    the earth, the skyline. Numb
    today & so am I. I am too
    thin. Built like I won't explode
    on hot afternoons, a mirror
    to the sky. My body is a hurt
    where tall grasses grow, where
    clouds pass, where rain sinks.
    It aches where I touch
    the ground.

The prairies are split:
        into farmland,
        plots. Locked
        in the control of continuity
        & destruction. A plaque
        of canola on my arm itches.
        I want to scratch.

I can't explain how I feel today.

The wish for winter. Every season
an emergency, distinct but repeating
like the bones of my rib cage
or prairie highways in blowing snow.

I am the outline of a person:
                    flat,
                    alone. On the shoulder
                    heading west, formed into black
                    plastic trash bags. I am still
                    too heavy for the wind
                    to take me anywhere fast.

I am still too much.

IT IS AND IT IS

After & for Selina Boan

in a dream there is a field where time has no hands to hold our bodies.
we crawl on grass crystalized to our skin entering new & old phases of
matter, the fast & then dull ache of bones aging back & forth in our
shared time glitter like clear light over clear water & i have no words to
describe abundance beyond the absence of fear. in a dream is a dream
where time is noose-less, rendered into a strip of masking tape keeping
flowers pressed in an old book, the words given new meaning under
petals & the concept of preservation. renewal is a beast we have braided
in our hair twice just to get a feel for it. small teeth & incisors keep
falling out of our mouths, always replaced, old & new to bite at any
sight of an edge to this hour. this field is fenceless & upside down & deep
with black soil where we bury ash that smells like the future, ash that
smells like the past. is it medicine? the infinite? the circular? where we
both make words out of the same damn world over & over again. i hope
so & i tell you that before we walk home. i tell you that before we are
real again.

THE ACADEMY ASKS FOR CONTEXT

I

The box of cellophane is on fire. Tips over in the attic.
Catches on the dresses that hang in my gaze, my gaze
on fire too. Continuity. This is my line of sight, a
touch of the feminine, something too hot to hold. I wait for
the end of the book where I am turned into a princess, when
my clothes aren't rags anymore, rages & rages & rages.
My mother won't read fast enough for me to get there tonight.

II

Water can put a fire out but skin gets hypothermic
when it's burned deep enough. I learned
that from my sister. A story is a rock formation I chip
away at. Throw the story in the Red River, throw myself
in the river. My mother would swim there when
she was young but it's too polluted
now. It was too polluted then. But she didn't care.

III

I call my youth worker a bitch & take my medicine.
She does my laundry while I combust on the couch.
Some people say you can see my age in my hands
so I wear black gloves, never cut my fingernails,
bite them off at night. I tell the shadows I need fifteen
dollars for cigarettes. They tell me to *fuck off* & so I dream
I smoke on the banks of the river, throw my butts in the water,
& the shadows ask *Where is your mother?*

IV

I will die on a boat in the river with my father. A medicine man
told him he'd die in water but my mother doesn't believe in all that.
She still makes me smudge the basement when she thinks
a ghost lives there & we walk to the bridge where my future
brother will attempt to die when he is sixteen. I am a child
& I will throw myself off the bridge too. It is big & blue
& surely the river will catch me.

v

I have no connection to the stars. I am all fluid & robust
rivers where bodies float or burn depending on the day. My father's
boat leaves oil slicks on the surface & I dip my hands in them,
eat oil, get sick. I throw up over the side & rock to my
mother's voice telling me to *SHUT THE FUCK UP* while I gag.
I did this to myself. I did it to spite you.

THE TICK

Grandpa yells my name & it spills
        on the ground like a bucket of pickerel.
My name is written on the tag of a dirty dress, pulled
        from discards & initialled in Sharpie. I wear
the histories of my cousins & I don't want to help them clean
        fish. Metal basin where my mother was bathed, where I
am bathed, head checked for ticks
        with matches at hand. I don't know how to swim, but I know
how to run in the field before tick season
        dies—fat, bloody. One digs into my skin
like I'm a fish being pulled to shore, anchored
        by its head in my head. I already have a reputation.
I'm already afraid. My blood & the blood of deer
        before me. A history of it. A story I have told
myself, have made my mother tell me at night.

AKI

this country has a name & it is no
father no clear sky no blue
on the horizon that is the bank
of a river run at the lip
of the earth no memory in dirt
I track into the tent pitched
by the side of the road no
godly blessing on this camp no
man here to fuck my mother sideways
& leave with three good years & two priors
no rcmp no gunpowder no marginalia
no notes at all in my book of no
knowledge an echo from sparse
trees spruce shakes birch leans
toward the sun my voice caught in the smoke
from burning fields I would kill
for a cigarette some gasoline to light
both & fall asleep finally warm

COUGAR ALERT

I went snowshoeing no one

       told me about the cougar in the woods

I should be back before sunset

       the snow to my knees the cold froze

my eyelashes little hooks I blinked

       & got fastened to I pretended

I conquered these lands

       not understanding I was the object

of the conquering I was a child

       who couldn't remember a time before

Mother lay in bed silent not asleep

       but staring at the past in the walls

a time before Grandmother would dance

       until she fell drunk & not happy but not

unhappy not anything at all except her love

     for me I remember I asked for a drink

& she offered me vodka I wanted orange juice

     but I drank with her twelve years old

back from the woods cougar alert

     on the radio

BRAID

My grandma never had her hair cut
by nuns or Indian agents.

She chooses a tight perm now, bald
spots from where she tugs on it

when she's drunk, pulling memories
from her head. As a child she cleaned

houses for whites off-reserve, permitted
once a day to go to Selkirk, East Selkirk,

places she would live when she grew up.
Her hair was long back then, like mine

now, black, straight as prairie
highway. It's red today. She covers

the greys with Vidal Sassoon boxed dye,
rusts under the shower cap

as I roll cigarettes for her at the kitchen
table. I love when she touches

my hair, compares
our faces. I look nothing like her.

THE SELKIRK JOURNAL ARCHIVE

My namesake is deep red, burgundy, brandy
rust on his lips. In Red Rose tea, in white
Pyrex glass, at the Lord Selkirk
Hotel we simply call God. He
& his friend, Natives, like spruce
trees, have skin hard as bark. Both are arrested
drinking off-reserve. Caged, kept in the drunk tank
overnight with handcuffs that bite like barn
cats. Off-reserve is a plot of land in East
Selkirk. He fishes beside it with a silver-and-bone
flask in his shirt. His hands smell like bait
& tobacco & my grandma's
perfume. He ownerships, sells fish
wholesale, & raises seventeen kids
with the profits. Drinking off-reserve,
he & his friend, Natives, like pickerel,
alcohol to numb the currents of the Red River. His blue
boat, his brown nets, his red skin, all flattened
in the prairie sun. Sheen of sweat, a hangover,
he wakes up in the clothes he wore
yesterday. Twenty-two dollars & thirty cents
to the judicial body, for the burn through his body,
a privilege to lose himself like I'm lost. We live
in each other's veins. I feel it in a shot
of whiskey, the tree his ashes are spread
under. Today that tree is on private property. I sing
"A Mansion on the Hill." I ownership & drink
at the Lord. I ownership & trespass.

WHEN YOU FIND OUT THE BOY YOU FIRST KISSED IS DEAD

you are in a bed that's not your own reading his obituary in the *Winnipeg Free Press*. You learn that obituaries are apolitical by design. They hide our real positions, they hide our faces. This obituary hides that this boy died from an overdose, that he was poisoned by the state, that he would still be alive with safe supply. You find out because you Google his name + your hometown, ask your sister who still lives there & she knows all the gossip, the good stuff, & find out he's been an addict for years. You don't know how to feel, startled by an emptiness. You think about your cousin who died the same way, your other cousin who took her own life, & you are grotesque in your remembering. You unfeel, numb like an object, the hairbrush on your side table. The boy you first kissed leaves behind his sister & his brother, his mother & his father & you think about the word *leaves*, as if he had the choice to stay & just didn't want to make it. You think about the times you made the choice to leave, half-hearted, always dragging yourself to the ER because truthfully you were afraid to die. You just wanted someone to know you were alive. *See*, you think. *See me*. & you bring this boy's death back to yourself because you don't know how to anticipate your reactions. What if your sisters die? Your father? What if you die in your sleep, unknowing, & there is nothing afterwards? You think of a kiss so chaste & underwhelming you barely remember you did it.

LOVE LETTER TO SOUTHERN AUTHORITY

Southern Authority means no father, no mother. Means nobody. A permanent ward, fauna in the background, a deer, a moose, myself. I stand at the door of a new home & don't knock. Beyond it are fields to graze in, trees to rub my soft flesh against, shake off the flies. I don't know what exists inside, the bones of it are slimy & white like teeth, the foundation growing concrete like skin over a burn. The doorknob blisters when I grab it. I choose to walk away, hands at my sides, afraid to touch even a crocus. Everything I grasp recoils, transforms. Every novelty is terrifying & I am still so young. Birds fly toward me, circle, & dive. They pluck out my old eyes & replace them with birch bark. I live for a hundred years like this. No one can tell the difference.

ODE TO NANABUSH

Mother, Father, bingo caller.
Friday nights on Peguis First
Nation. Call out to me. Night-
hawk, grey rabbit
on the flood plain, the quills
of porcupines left on the side
of the highway north past
Winnipeg. Boozhoo, I ask
for you in the snakepits
of Narcisse, pits ripe
with the memory of when
you created Earth against
their writhing bodies, black
as scorch marks on stone. You
are neolithic, red ochred, eaten
as I say my name aloud
with the shadow of artifice
against a white screen. Will I
find you listening? In the bottom
of my can of beer, drinking
you in, a snare. I know the rez
was a prison first & then a home
in name, if not in body, if not
in my hands. Were you a prisoner
too? Or did you slide in moon-
light over fences, over walls, over
city girls awake at three a.m., the ones

like me who aren't like prophets,
who never remember their dreams?

1999

After Liz Howard

recollect a glacial lake in the eye
of mother standing in the fan
of lake agassiz wide hands
on my back against the wind of a
levelled plain canticle fertile valley
synchronicity of silt & water
split into three by rivers & me cold
ply of fingers on my sister
against walls of neon vlt
gamble of glacier water prairie
noise nickel-plated satisfaction of
rise of ice on the riverbank & mother's
seasons measured by quarters running
low who knows her habits who knows
where she'll be tomorrow my face
reflected in hers so alike in water
porous plump identical

MANITOBA

straits of manitou off
the horizon red river
valley written on my father's
back hydrography lines fresh
water unread like prehistory
rain down his shoulders
hiss torrential voices of
his two daughters as he walks
away this is the red in spring-
time it thaws slowly & then
faster a father ice floe a father
water faceless inside the river-
bed melting like a body
into another body & coursing
north like all rivers here

PICKEREL

mother is sharp
as her
father's filleting knife
a blade with eyes
cutting pickerel
into short strips
on the kitchen table
smell of dead fish
immovable a subsistence
& the edges of my mother
grind as she becomes points
hangs fish
from her limbs
in cigarette smoke
particleboard walls stained
dead with nicotine
I breathe in
& blur at her knees
a danger
crisis of rot & preservation
in the two-room shack
where she was raised
I touch scales
of discarded fish & pour
vinegar on my hands
it stings the cuts
from the last time

she held them
a threat in me bleeding
the fish bloody too

ALL BLUE AND ALL BRITTLE

A girl can fit inside a fist.
I was curled up in one,
in ammonite found on Pine Creek
First Nation. In a field
of canola, in a graveyard
on the rez, in a glass bottle. I could be
sixteen again. Pray my eyes bloodshot,
look directly at God or the sun
except I never really believed
in anything but my own needs.
I want to be held by someone
fuller than I am. Hold
onto what I have like my mother's
hand on my bony jaw. She once racked
my mouth open with a bar
of Ivory soap & I spat out water
from Lake Winnipegosis. I didn't
understand the lake well enough
to interpret what I'd said. I'm saying
anything to anyone now, spun
around because every horizon
looks the same. They're all blue
& the sky is a bruise
that futures on my palms. This violence
is quiet, has no body except my body
which is to say I will let the sky
silence me. Did I learn anything

from my ancestors? Can I twist my mouth
open against the clouds? Let me fall
& fossilize at the bottom
of the lake. Let my body brittle. Let it break
off in pieces in other people's hands.

WHAT JOY?

Name me a love
    name. A name with feathers picked from sidewalks & bound
      with twine. Create

a body
    of hollows & let me fill them with glass beads & cigarettes. Name me
      my father & the story

he orates when he's drunk
    on the balcony. Talk about wisdom, a noble bottle of brandy, etymology
      of family, Foncine, Delaronde,

Bird & Ratte. Break
    all family names into pieces & watch them turn into stones
      I throw into Lake Winnipeg.

Watch me turn to stone
    or a pillar of salt, other words for still, silent. Other words for weathering
      the way we love.

We are nothing if not forgiving.

NOTES

Thank you to all the editors who had a part in the previous publication of these poems:

"Poem for White People" was published in *ARC Poetry Magazine*.
"Ode to Diabetes" was published in *Catapult*.
"The All + Flesh" and "A Glossary of Illness" were published in *CV2*.
"The Tick" was published in *Brick*.
"Braid" was published in *The Ex-Puritan*.
"Love Letter to Southern Authority" and "The Selkirk Journal Archive" were published in *The Fiddlehead*.
"19," "Aki," "Ode to Nanabush," "1999," "Manitoba," and "Pickerel" were published in some form by Rahila's Ghost Press in my chapbook *I Am Still Too Much*.

ACKNOWLEDGEMENTS

Thank you to Liz Bachinsky, the first person who ever told me I was a poet.

Thank you to Billy-Ray Belcourt and Sheryda Warrener, who both guided me to a world where poetry is possible.

Thank you to Selina Boan, my first editor, my poetry twin, and someone who always answers my phone calls.

Thank you to my love, Heather Saluti, who is holding my hand. We make joy out of all the complexities.

Thank you to Mallory Tater and Curtis LeBlanc of Rahila's Ghost Press, who saw me reading at the Heatley, decided to publish my chapbook, and then immediately became my wonderful friends.

Thank you to Christopher Evans for his care with my words.

Thank you to Sage Hill Writing, the Banff Centre, the British Columbia Arts Council, and the Canada Council for the Arts for their support in writing this book.

Thank you to Karen Solie, Jordan Abel, and Eduardo C. Corral, who had first eyes on many of these poems.

Thank you to House of Anansi Press and to my editor, Kevin Connolly, for helping me grow this book.

Thank you to all my friends who listen to me agonize and who themselves inspire me: Jess, Molly C.B., Molly S., Amanda, Jas, Mica, Carter, Jocelyn, Rachel, Emily, Shaun, Megan, Micah, jaye, Justin, Cara N., Cara M., Whess, Matt, Df, Erin, Vance, Richard, Sam, Dinah, Kate, Jasmine, Paisley, Kyle, Dallas, Conor, Adele, and Annick.

Thank you to all the friends I made on LiveJournal, the ones who have kept in touch fifteen years strong.

And thank you to my family, every one of you. Even when our relationships are hard, know that I wrote this book for us.

BRANDI BIRD is an Indigiqueer Saulteaux, Cree, and Métis writer from Treaty 1 territory. They currently live and learn on the land of the Squamish, Tsleil-Waututh, and Musqueam peoples. Their chapbook *I Am Still Too Much* was published by Rahila's Ghost Press in Spring 2019 and they have been published in *Poetry Is Dead*, *Room Magazine*, *Brick Magazine*, *Prism International* and others. They work as a freelance editor and workshop facilitator, and they study Creative Writing at the University of British Columbia. They enjoy listening to the same song over and over again and love their three ancient cats, Babydoll, Burt, and Etta.